Untypical ZEEKE

Written by
Rossana Hahn

Illustrated by
Nadia Ronquillo

$$e^{i\pi} + 1 = 0$$

To every single one
of my wonderful and
talented students.

You truly have superpowers.
Also, to Pete.

I am Zeeke and
this is my cat Smiles.
We do a lot of things together.

We watch TV together.

6

We take
walks together.

We even go to sleep together.

8

We do many things together,
except for one...

Smiles doesn't go to
school with me...

but I wish he could.

I like going to school.
Science is my favorite subject.

I love learning about Animals
and doing experiments!

But when we start reading,
everything goes south!

I'm not good at reading
and that makes me mad.

Most of the time I end up
screaming and crying.

Sometimes I rock my body back
and forth to calm myself down,
and that makes me feel better.

I know my friends get bothered when I act like that, but I just can't help it.

I was born
with autism
and expressing my feelings
when I'm frustrated
is hard for me.

$e^{i\pi} + 1 = 0$

Kids with autism
are like any other kid,
our brain just
works differently.

I have a great memory
and I'm really good at drawing...
especially dinosaurs.

My friend Katy also has autism,
she is the best reader in her class.

My teacher says that
having autism
is like having
superpowers!

Except there are times
when it doesn't feel like that.

I can't stand
loud noises
or strange smells!

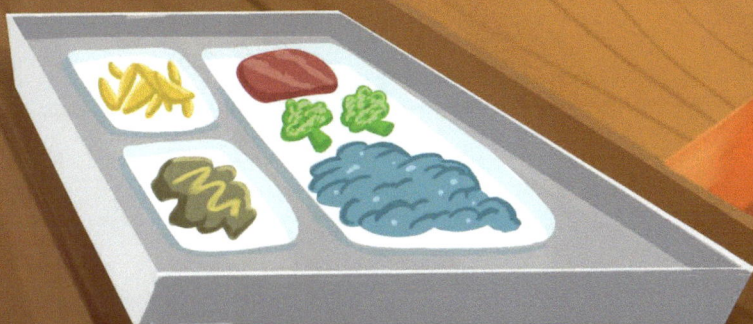

There are times when
other kids laugh or stare at me,
and that makes me sad.

I wish they could understand
that even if I act different at times,
I am just like them.

I have dreams.

I have a family.

And I have feelings too.

I'm sure one day they'll see
that I'm just like them.

Then, maybe I won't miss
my cat Smiles as much.

"Wanting to be free.
Wanting to be me.
Trying to make people see.
And accept the real me."
Scott Lentine

www.ingramcontent.com/pod-product-compliance
Lightning Source LLC
Chambersburg PA
CBHW041551040426
42447CB00002B/139